500

MW01482369

Copyright © 2008
Paper Russells, LLC

ISBN 978-1440447754

MANTRAS

ANCIENT WISDOM
FOR SOLVING
LIFE'S EVERYDAY PROBLEMS

Shashvatananda

Contents

Introduction
Mantras and Me

When I was around 11 years old, our school took a bus trip to the local library. While most of the children were off exploring the wonders of Nancy Drew and the Hardy Boys for some reason I found myself in the Philosophy and Religion section.

I recall pulling a book off the shelf seemingly for no particular reason and opening it directly to an old black and white photograph of the Portola Palace in Lhasa Tibet. At that moment it was as if all my breath was sucked out of me and my mind went totally quiet, and somewhere in the depth of my being I knew I was looking at a very familiar place one that once I may have called home. I just stood there for a very long time and stared at that photograph.

Then hurriedly like a starving man having a fine meal laid before him I began to devour the book. When it was time to leave and head back to school I took the book with me to check out. It was a pitched battle, my teacher and the librarian on one side and one very determined boy on the other. In the end I got to take the book home.

This book changed my life and I began a life long pursuit for spiritual insight and knowledge. In its pages were descriptions of a world rarely seen. A woman who spent many years witnessing a society known only by rumor and speculation wrote the book. Here was an eyewitness account of what at the time I took to be real magic.

With this book combined with an unexplained inward knowing of the place, its customs; rights, and knowledge I wholeheartedly began reading everything I could get my hands on about Tibet its culture and teachings. And, I began, in my ignorance, what I deduced as a meditation practice.

This practice was quite complex and involved sitting quietly in the lotus posture with my spine straight while emptying my mind of everything. I would do this at night after having gone to bed or during the day when no one else was home. As you might imagine it was very difficult, however after some time I was able to, for short periods of time, achieve a state with gaps in my thought pattern.

Then it happened. After practicing my meditation for around four years whenever I could one day I was sitting doing my practice when the bottom dropped out. No mind no thought, and when I came back, so to speak, there was the most amazing feeling of bliss. This Bliss we might describe as happiness without a reason or "the peace which passeth understanding".

I didn't know it at the time but I had transcended and experienced the basis of all life that which is complete fullness yet contains nothing.

The problem was my meditation practice was extremely difficult and required great effort and time to achieve the effortless state. I began to search for something easier. My readings lead me to try Zen, which, while intellectually satisfying yielded no repetition of the mindless state. I tried several other practices and even religions until one day I received a phone call that was to be another turning point in my life.

My best friend had gone off collage and suggested that I leave my job with the Forest Service and continue my education.

I arrived on campus to find Maharishi Mahesh Yogi teaching a course about meditation and training young men and woman like me how to teach Transcendental Meditation (TM), a mantra based meditation practice.

I knew I had found what I was looking for in my first meditation. Upon learning I experienced quite easily that state of mindlessness I had been struggling so hard for.

I knew for certain that TM worked for me when I was walking down the street feeling the perfect bliss within yet realizing that nothing what so ever had happened in my life save for meditation to make it so.

Within six months of beginning the practice I had gone from a 1.28 GPA to a 4.0, typical of TM practitioners, and had made the decision to become a TM Teacher.

I became a teacher of TM in 1972 and have taught TM since then. I am extremely grateful to Maharishi for all his teachings and wisdom that have shaped my life.

Needless to say my interest in mantras and how they may help our lives has continued to this day.

But why meditate; what is this mindless state, and why is it such a good thing? How does and why does it work, what are the benefits, and who should do it, and of course how?

These are important questions for the seeker of
spiritual truth though for the most part beyond
the scope of this book. What can be said here is
that the truth lies within us and cannot be
found in the pages of any work no matter how
great. Words can, however, point to that truth.

Included in this brief book many mantras are
referenced but none of them come from the
Transcendental Meditation program. If you
have the desire to learn TM please seek a
qualified teacher.

What is a Manta?

The use of mantras is quite likely as old as human existence. In one form or another people have been using mantras to help their daily lives for centuries.

American Indians used mantra like chanting to help in finding food and for protection. Many indigenous cultures have uncovered various mantras like methods, but perhaps the formal beginning started in India several thousand years ago when the great seers, called Rishis, began to cognize the workings of our universe.

A mantra is for the most part a lever; a way to work directly with cause and effect. It is something you can do to create an effect that you want; one that benefits you. Mantras fix things. The Mantras found here were originally formulated in the Shastric language, which we know today as Sanskrit.

Mantras fall into two basic categories those that are for spiritual use and advancement, and those that are used for resolving day-to-day living issues such as curing snakebite or to become a more loving person.

All mantras will in the larger sense help us along our chosen spiritual path. This then raises the often-asked question of whether or not there may be some conflict between the use of mantras and our spiritual or religious path? The answer to that lies in what your personal belief system is.

If you believe in God and see God as Omnipotent, Omnipresent, and Omniscient then you should have no problem with mantras for your path is inclusive. Mantras then are prayers, supplications to God for our well-being. They are prayers designed to have a specific outcome, prayers that have withstood the test of time.

Mantras are tools for helping us live our lives more fully, mitigating our difficulties while enhancing the positive aspects.

On the next page is an example of a mantra written in Devanagari the script used to write Sanskrit. This is one of the most revered and famous of mantras used by millions of people daily. We'll give a pronounceable version later in the book.

The Gayatri Mantra

ॐ भूर्भुवः स्वः ।
तत् सवितुर्वरेण्यं ।
भर्गो देवस्य धीमहि ।
धियो यो नः प्रचोदयात् ॥

Gayatri Translation

Om
Bhu = earth
Bhuvas = atmosphere
Svar = light
Tat = that
Savitur devasya = sun deity
Varenyam = desirable
Bhargo = radiance
Devasya = divine
Dhimahi = may we attain
Dhiyah nah = our prayers
Yah pracodayat = who may stimulate

The Practice of
Using Mantras

Each mantra has a set of rules to follow these
are generally simple; however they should be
adhered to if the desired results are to bear fruit.

Each mantra must be done for a specific number
of days and for a specified number of repetitions each day. Most are done for 40 days 108
times each day. It is best to do the mantra at
the same time each day if possible.

It is important to establish a quiet place for this
practice and to set a time for it. It is best to
not be disturbed, so you may want to let other
people know that you prefer not to be disturbed
and perhaps take the phone off the hook.

If for any reason you are interrupted, you should start over again and recount the repetitions. If you miss a day you must also start over again at the beginning of the 40-day process or required number of days. If you are doing more then one mantra that mantra should be restarted at the beginning though you may continue with others in succession.

When you begin the process start by chanting the mantra out loud then when you feel comfortable with your pronunciation and memorization you repeat the mantra internally to yourself; mentally. Until you have the mantra memorized it is best to keep a written copy to refer to in front of you while practicing.

For counting the mantra, using a mala or rosary is easiest. Malas have either 108 beads plus one additional out from the strand, or half malas have 54 beads. This makes counting easy. You can wear the mala when not using it for counting though it should be removed for bathing and intimate relations.

When using the mala start at the extra bead (called the Meru or Guru bead) traditionally the first finger (index finger) is not used in counting with a mala, rather you pull the beads over your ring finger with your thumb to count. Just keep the first two fingers out of the way.

It is best to hold your intention for the desired results prior to each session. Some people have found it useful to write down their desire/intention on a piece of paper and read it before starting then when you have completed the 40 days light a candle and burn the paper.

Have an open heart and faith in the process, and if at the end of the prescribed number of days you feel like you are not quite where you would like to be then begin another set, start counting again – redo the process. It is possible that some large block of Karma must be removed to bring about success. Some more time may be needed. Don't lose faith if at the first try you are having some difficulty. Just keep at your practice. In time the benefits will manifest in your life.

It is common for people to have various physical sensations either during or after the mantra practice and you might feel some tiredness. These are signs of success – it is working.

More is not necessarily better. It is better not to over do mantra usage. Instead we trust and stay with the prescribed practice for best results.

17

Mantras
For
Relationships

Most of us would like to have a relationship with the "right" person. But how do we find him or her?

Dating services abound, single bars haven't gone out of business, fishing off the company pier is still acceptable to many, but let's face it getting the desired results seem to be just a matter of luck. I know one woman who went at it like a business process; she dated over 250 men in a year's time sometimes two or three a week before she found her "Mr. Right".

Using a mantra may help. You can shape the process of finding the right partner, and you may well find the perfect person, perhaps a soul mate.

But, know what you want, not a whole laundry list full of every specific and intimate detail. Keep it simple, for example "I want to be with someone spiritual" or "The qualities of kindness and generosity are important to me".

Be open and not judgmental to those who begin to show up in your life. You might just get what you have longed for.

Mantra
for
Women to find
the
Right Man

Sat Patim Dehi
Parameshwara

Pronounced:

Sawt Pawteem Dayhe Pa-ram-esh-warah

Mantra
for
Men to Find
the
Right Woman

Om Shrim Shriyei Namaha

Pronounced:

Om Shreem Shreeyea Nah-ma-ha

Mantra
for a
Blissful Marriage

Om Radha Krishnaya Namaha

Pronounced:

Om Rodhaa Krishnlyah Nah-ma-ha

*Mantra
to bring Exceptional
Love to Your Life*

Om Parama Prema Rupaiya Namaha

Pronounced:

Om Parrawmah Praymah Roupieyah Nah-ma-ha

Mantra
for you
to be Love Itself

Aham Prema

Pronounced:

Ah-hah-m Prayma

Mantras
for
Relationship
Problem Solving

You are in a relationship and you are basically good with that, but there are the rough spots the tough times. We all go through it, but why not help smooth out the rough spots if we can.

Try these mantras for healing and understanding. Using the right mantra can make a difference, it may take some time but like all good things in life it is worth the effort.

Mantra
to Resolve Problems
in a Relationship

Hrim Shrim Klim
Parameshwari Swaha

Pronounced:

Hreem Shreem Kleem
Pah-ram-mesh-warre Swaha

Mantra
for
Promoting
Understanding in a
Relationship

Om Sharavana Bhavaya Namaha

Pronounced:

Om Sharavahnah Bhavayah
Na-ma-ha

Mantas
for
Illness and Disease

Getting a Healthy
Mind and Body

Sometimes we just get sick while some people
are hit hard with a debilitating disease.

Thousands of years ago in India it is said that
the village doctor's livelihood was dependent on
whether or not the people in his care became ill.
How then did they manage to keep their jobs?

The answer lies in prevention, preventative medical treatment. This involved diet, nutrition, and right living, but it also centered on the use of mantras. Over time a great knowledge evolved that helped not only reduce the incidence of medical issues but also helped cure them when they arose.

This ancient science of health is called Ayurveda. Ayurvedic medicine is the basis for Chinese and Tibetan Medicine and its tenets are practiced daily by millions of people. The word Ayurveda means something close to "The Knowledge of Long Life".

The Ayurvedic mantras are about health. They are specifically designed to give relief from a host of medical, mental, and daily life issues. Do they work? Many people have found relief and even cure from difficult illness and disease. As you begin to use these healing mantras it is also wise to seek the advice of a competent medical practitioner.

Ayurvedic medicine is a large subject and covers many aspects relating to the overall value of having and living a healthy life. Presented within the body of Ayurvedic knowledge is the subject of Vastu or Vastushastra the science of architecture for healthy living.

There is a delightful story about the use of Ayurvedic knowledge in the great Indian epic the Ramayana. The Ramayana in its present form dates from perhaps 500 BCE (12,000 years ago according to Vedic Astrology) and has some 24,000 verses. Principally it is the story of a great hero Rama and his adventures to gain back his lost kingdom.

One sub story involves Hanuman who is the King of the monkeys. Rama needs a very special herb to heal his brother who is in grave danger of dying but the herb only grows far away in the north of India. Rama asks Hanuman to please go and fetch the herb called Sanjivani that has the power save Rama's brother's life. Hanuman being the epitome of loyalty just leaps up and using his mystical powers makes himself very big so he can go to the Himalayas in just a few steps. Once he arrives he realizes that he has no idea of what the Sanjivani herb looks like... what to do?

Being at that point very large he realizes the simple solution. He just reaches down and picks up the entire mountain where the herb grows and carries it back to Rama.

Taking the Sanjivani herb and using his knowledge of Ayurvedic medicine Rama cures his brother and the story continues.

Mantra
for
Reducing Fever

Om Vindhya Vanana Hum Fat Swaha

Pronounced:

Om Vin-dah-yah Va-nah-nah Hoom
F-ah-t Swah-hah

Mantra
for
Removing Disease

Om Shrim Hrim Klim Aim Indakshyai Namah

Pronounced:

Om Shreem Hreem Kleem I'm Indah-kash-yea
Na-ma-ha

Mantra
for
Good Health

Achyutam Chamritam Chaiva Japedoushadhakarmani

Pronounced:

Auch-you-tam Chamm-ri-tam Chai-vah
Jap-ee-doous-haud-ha-car-mah-nee

Mantra
for
Sound Sleep

Om Agasti Shayinah

Pronounced:

Om Ag-astee Sha-ee-nah

Mantra
for
Healing the Eyes

Om Grinihi Suryaya Adityom

Pronounced:

Om Grih-nee-hee Suor-yah-yah
Ah-deat-yohmm

Mantras
To
Help Manage
Our Psychology

Managing fear and anger are part of daily life.
These mantras can help build our confidence,
remove negativity, and even help create good luck.

We can find help for managing depression
and anxiety, becoming more cheerful and
reversing sorrow.

This group of mantras also helps us find inner peace, creates peace in our environment, and helps us to be more compassionate.

Some may be useful in removing or reducing addiction and give help in getting rid of unwanted desires.

Mantra
for
Getting out of
Sadness

Om Sarva Dukha Haraya Namaha

Pronounced:

Om Sahr-vah Dook-hah-rah-yah Nah-ma-ha

Mantra
for
Cheerfulness

Om Prasannatmane Namaha

Pronounced:

Om Prah-sahn-aht-mah-neh
Nah-ma-ha

Mantra
to
Help Manage Depression
and Anxiety

Om Shrun-kala Bandha Mochakaya Namaha

Pronounced:

Om Shroon-kah-lah Bahn-dhah Mo-chah-kah-yah Nah-ma-ha

Mantra
for
Help in Difficult
Situations

Om Klim Kalika-yei Namaha

Pronounced:

Om Kleem Kah-lee-kah-yea Nah-ma-ha

Mantra
for
Living a Life Based
on Truth

Om Satyei Namaha

Pronounced:

Om Saht-yea Nah-ma-ha

Mantra
for
Removing Unwanted
Desire

Om Nishka Mayei Namaha

Pronounced:

Om Neesh-kah Mah-yea Nah-ma-ha

Mantra
to
Remove Depression

Om Bhoginyei Namaha

Pronounced:

Om Bhoh-geen-yea Nah-ma-ha

Mantra
to
Help Fulfill Our
Desires

Om Kama Dayinyei Namaha

Pronounced:

Om Kah-mah Dah-een-yea Nah-ma-ha

Mantra
for
Confidence
and Inner Strength

Om Eim Hrim Klim Chamundayei Vichei Namaha

Pronounced:

Om I'm Hreem Kleem
Chah-moon-dah-yea Vee-cheh
Na-ma-ha

Mantra
for
Removal of
Negative Forces and for
Protection

Narasimha Ta Va Da So Hum

Pronounced:

Nah-rah-seem-ha Tah Vah Dah Soh Huhm

50

What is Yoga?

In the west the word Yoga often conjures up pictures of people seemingly bending their bodies into pretzels in various states of undress, or perhaps some half naked man lying on a bed of nails.

The word Yoga means to join together, to yoke, and to unite. It is generally accepted that this is referring to a coming together with God, a uniting with the Divine.

The subject of Yoga is divided into two fundamental divisions that of Yoga and that of Sankhya. Or we could say of Experience/Action on one side of the equation and of Knowledge on the other. The ideal is for the yoga practitioner under the direction of his or her teacher to first be given an experience and then knowledge about that experience.

When you think about it this makes perfect sense for how better to learn then by experience and have an explanation given that not only explains but also enlightens the mind.

The philosophy of Yoga is quite extensive and complex. It is said that there are 108 holy ways to transcend and reach higher consciousness and 8 unholy ways. The unholy ways are processes that involve the use of drugs, mortification of the flesh, alcohol, certain sexual practices, and various forms of magic. These unholy processes are very difficult and more often than not lead to failure and a life destroyed. The holy practices generally have long traditions and an easily traceable succession of teacher masters.

True teachers of yoga have no egos, take full responsibility for their student disciples and are full of great love and heart.

It is possible to say with some degree of accuracy that there are only two true spiritual paths one of effort and the other being effortless. Maharishi once said that we must "move God to move us" by this we may infer that we are for the most part responsible for our spiritual lives. Through devotion in our daily practice of Yoga we may begin to enhance and enjoy real spirituality.

To walk the effortless path is rare for it involves a Master taking personal responsibility of our spiritual evolution. This path is called effortless because we are called to just be in a state of surrender and complete trust while the Master moves us forward. On this rare and beautiful path we may suffer greatly in the process but usually only for a relatively short period of time. Of course that may be many years by our unenlightened reckoning.

Regardless of the path Yoga is about union with the divine. In the Vedic literature we are told that true spiritual evolution begins with enlightenment, and it is then that we become able to help others along their paths.

Seed Mantras

These mantras are the core of all mantras and the basis from which according to the Vedas all language springs. They are called Bija mantras. Bija means Seed.

These word/letters are then combined to form words that are considered to have great power. Each of the mantras represents a specific form of energy or Deva.

The language of consciousness is symbolic. It is contextual and conceptual. If you describe something with these words it is possible to know it in its entirety, if you have the right state of consciousness. Perhaps you have heard the statement that "In the beginning there was the word." From the Vedic perspective the "word" is the fundamental building block(s) of the creation.

This group of mantra is often used to represent Chakras or centers of energy within the human physiology and is generally pictured as lotus flowers.

There are seven major Chakras these are:

1. Muldhara
2. Svadhisthana
3. Manipuran
4. Anahata
5. Vissudha
6. Ajana
7. Sahasara

A Bija mantra is associated with each petal on the lotus. It takes a great Master to help the student clear each chakra. The practice of doing so should not be undertaken without proper guidance.

The Anahata is the heart chakra. By clearing the Anahata it is said that all the other chakras become cleared as well.

There are individual Bija mantras for each of the seven chakras though it is a bit more complex each chakra having many sounds associated with it. These basic chakra mantras are (in order of association with its chakra):

1. LAM
2. VAM
3. RAM
4. YAM
5. HAM
6. OM
7. AH or Silence

Some other Bija mantras are associated with the various Deva such as Haum, which is considered to have a connection with Shiva and Dum representing Durga. Gam (pronounced Gum) connects with Ganesh the great remover of obstacles.

Narasimha who is considered to be an incarnation of Vishnu and half man half lion has one of the most unique of mantras – Kshraum pronounced something like shi-ram.

If you listen carefully to Vedic recitations you may hear many Bija mantras being sung one after the other. This is done to invoke the right atmosphere needed for the success of the Yoga or Vedic ceremony.

Famous Mantras

These are perhaps the most sacred and revered mantras of all, they have been in constant use from time immemorial.

We will begin with the Gayatri perhaps the most used mantra; it is regularly enjoined each morning at sunrise by millions of people each day around the world.

Gayatri Mantra

Om bhur bhuva suvaha
tat savitur varenyam
bhargo devasya dhimahi
dhiyo yonah prachadayat

The Gayatri Mantra is used every day by
millions of people in India to begin their day, a
morning prayer asking to have their life filled
with Divine Light.

Ganesh Mantra

Om suklam bharadharam vishnum seShivarnam chatur bhujamprasana vadanam dhyaiye sarva vighnopa Shantaye

Ganesh the son of Shiva is revered as the great remover of obstacles. Most Vedic ceremonies begin with a recitation in one form or another of the Ganesh mantras.

Prayer to the Guru

Om Gurur Brahma
Gurur Vishnur
Gurur Devo Maheshwara
Guruh Sakshat Param Brahma
Tasmi Shri Gurave Namaha

Om Akhanda Mandalakaram
Vyaptam Yena Characharam
Tat Padam Darshitam Yena
Tasmai Sri Gurave Namaha

This prayer is to one's Guru and the Guru of
all Gurus…

Sri Mrutyunajaya Mantra

Om Trayumbakam Yajamahe
Sughandhim Pushti Vardanam
Urvar-ukamiva Bandhanan
Mrityor Muksheeya Mamritat

This is perhaps the most famous, and greatest
healing mantra known throughout India...

Shiva Mantras

Om Nama Shivaya
Om Namo Shivaya

Lord Shiva represents the Creator and the Destroyer, he seems to have many personas but perhaps the most famous is that of the perfect Yogi sitting forever in silence and meditation.

Tibetan Mantra

Om Mani Padme Om

Perhaps the best-known mantra in the world,
meaning: Mani or mind and Padme or lotus
often translated as 'the jewel in the center of
the lotus'…

The Snake and The Rope

An ancient Vedic parable…

Once in a rural village in India a man began his usual early morning walk from the village to his field for the day's work. The morning's light was just beginning to shine and the world was still cast in shadows.

As the man walked along the rough path to the fields he was thinking about the work that lay before him, whether or not it would be the day to harvest the grain or to break the small dike and water once again.

Just as he was about to cross over into his field looking forward as the path stretched before him he saw something.

He paused, yes there was something, something out of place, just out from the edge of the forest lying in his way was a long curvy something.

Trying to clear his sleepy head, he could not quite make out what it was. Did it move, what could it be?

Then quite suddenly and with quite a startle he realized it must be a snake, a cobra no doubt. It was the right shape, and the right size. As he looked he was pretty sure it had moved. Quickly he backup thanking God he had not blindly stepped on it in the half light for if that had happened he knew for certain it would have be a quick and painful death.

Now his fear mounting he panicked, and with his heart pounding he turned and ran back to the village screaming the whole way SNAKE, SNAKE, SNAKE.

Needless to say when he arrived back at the village everyone was huddled by the village gate staring at him. What is it, what was the matter?

They tried in vain to calm the poor man; he was trembling so they knew there must be some grave danger. Finally, he was able to pull himself together enough to tell his fellow villagers about the snake the great cobra in the path to the field.

Are you sure, we haven't seen a snake in many years... Oh yes, it moved. And, so it was decided that a small group of the villagers would go with the man to investigate the snake.

Together the five biggest and bravest men along with the farmer hurried along the path to have a look. As they came closer to the spot the talk of snakes and stories of snakes became quite intense.

Then they were there, and sure enough so was the snake. They stood their mouths open their eyes wide and they just stared. Yes, indeed it seemed to move ever so snake like…

As the sun rose so too the shadows around the snake lengthened thus obscuring a clear view but they were sure what they saw. Now what to do?

After some considerably animated discussion it was decided to go to the village Priest and ask for guidance as he was considered to be the wisest man in the village.

Two men stayed to keep an eye on the snake and the rest went back to the village to meet with the Priest. The Priest having just finished the morning rituals in the temple was sitting down to his breakfast and about to bite into the lovely prepared meal his wife so honored him with each day when seemingly the whole village gathered at his door.

Whatever could be the cause for such a commotion the Priest wondered and he signaled for one of the men to enter. What is it that brings you and so many others to my door this morning my dear friend, the Priest said?

The man struggled to maintain his composure then carefully explained the situation asking the Priest what should be done.

Are you sure it is a snake? Yes, oh yes quite
sure. Well then it has been a good many years
since I have seen one. If it pleases you perhaps
you would be kind enough to take me to see
the great creature…

So off they went to see the snake with half
the village following along. After some time
they arrived at the place where the two villagers
had been left to keep an eye on the snake
and inquired as to what had taken place in
the meantime.

There it is the villagers said pointing to the
snake. The Priest looked and looked but as he
was old, had difficulty in making out the snake,
and being the ever practical man he was, he
walked toward the beast much to the amazement
of the villagers. Priest please be careful the
villagers called out, but even with these urgings
the Priest moved closer.

Finally the Priest stopped just a few feet from the snake and looking closely he began to laugh and laugh, and then turning back to the villagers he motioned for them to come closer. With fear and trepidation they inched nearer for such was their faith in the Priest. Once they were all standing together the Priest walked over to the snake and picked it up. Caring it back to the frightened villagers he simply said, "it is just a piece of rope", and soon everyone was enjoying a good laugh.

This is a parable about the powers of discrimination and discernment. To those with true clarity there are no illusions in life you can tell the difference between a piece of rope and a snake. You can discern truth from falsehood you can trust yourself to know right from wrong. Mantras help bring about higher levels of discrimination and discernment.

Mantras
for
Clarifying Our Lives

Here are the special mantras to increase inner and outer beauty and for becoming the spirit of truth.

A good friend who started working with the mantra for beauty shortly found herself being complemented on how healthy and happy she looked, her hair stylist even noted that her the condition of her hair was the best she had ever seen.

Mantra
for
Clearing the Mind

(To Think Clearly about what You Want)

Hung Vajra Peh

Pronounced:

Hoong Vahjra Pay

*Mantra for
Resolving Inner
Conflict and
Removing Obstacles*

Om Gum Ganapatayei
Namaha

Pronounced:

Om Gum Guh-nuh-puh-tuh-yea Nah-ma-ha

Mantra to Transform
the Energy of Fear

Shante Prashante Sarva Bhaya Upasha Mani Swaha

Pronounced:

Shan-the Prah-shan-the Sahr-vah
Bhah-yahOo-pah-shah Mah-nee Swah-ha

Mantra for
Spiritual Insight

Sat Chid Ekam Brahma

Pronounced:

Saht Cheed Eh-kahm Brah-mah

Mantra to Increase
Inner Beauty

Om Padma Sundharyei Namaha

Pronounced:

Om Pahd-mah Soon-dhar-yea Nah-ma-ha

Possible Experiences

What can happen when practicing mantras is a good and valid question. Mantras are a form of prayer but they are considered to be a prayer for a specific outcome.

The experience of transcendence or going beyond our regular experience of consciousness the waking, dreaming, and sleep states is one possible outcome. We could call this the experience of higher states of consciousness.

Generally higher states get divided into three or four depending on the teaching being given but that's another story.

For the mantras here the outcomes are, they work or they don't work for the practitioner. If they don't work it is most likely due to a lack of diligence and consistency of practice. Or, it is also possible that there may be some karmic block in the way of success. However, it should be noted that even the hardest rocks on the path of practice are often dissolved through love, grace, and faith in the teaching.

What should we expect then? Expect success, belay doubts, exercise faith, have patience with yourself, and don't give up.

A
Closing
Word

According to Vedic philosophy absolute surrender
to God is the key to a life free from suffering.
In the end by Grace we are left with only Love,
that which binds the boundless and creates the
universe that which is beyond all and is, in the
final analysis, is everything. It is by love that
creation manifests and through love that we are
rescued from ignorance. Love is the cosmic glue
that holds everything together.

Acknowledgements

Cover design by M. Speight
Cover Photo by C. Speight
Edited by George Baue

This book is dedicated to everyone seeking a life of love, light, and laughter.

I would like to acknowledge all those who are making a difference, who are helping recreate the world into a better place.

I give thanks for and to everyone who has made my life richer and fuller than I ever dreamed possible.

December 2008, by Shashvatananda

Made in the USA
Coppell, TX
09 February 2021